This book is written by

_____

You are good at

_____

You always help
me to

_____

I love when
you cook

_____

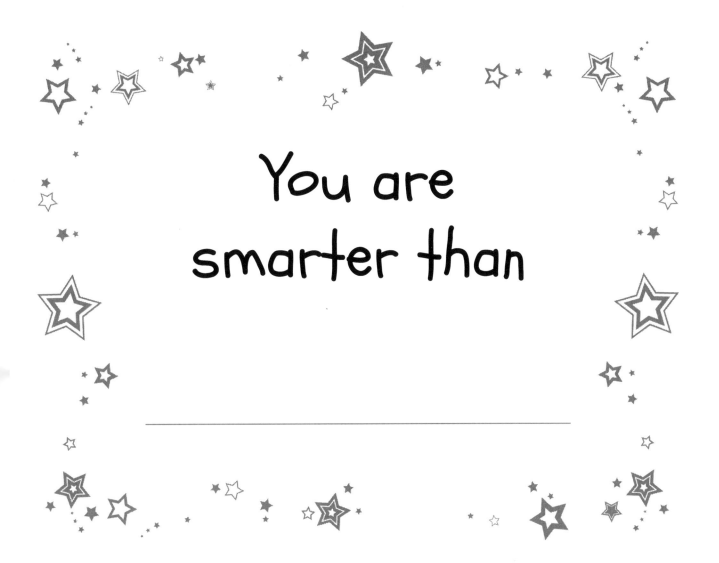

You are
smarter than

_____

My favorite thing
about you is

_____

If I had million bucks
I would buy you

_____

I like when you call me

_____

Our favorite thing to do together is

You are the happiest when

_____

Your favorite food is

_____

Tv show/movie that we both love is

_____

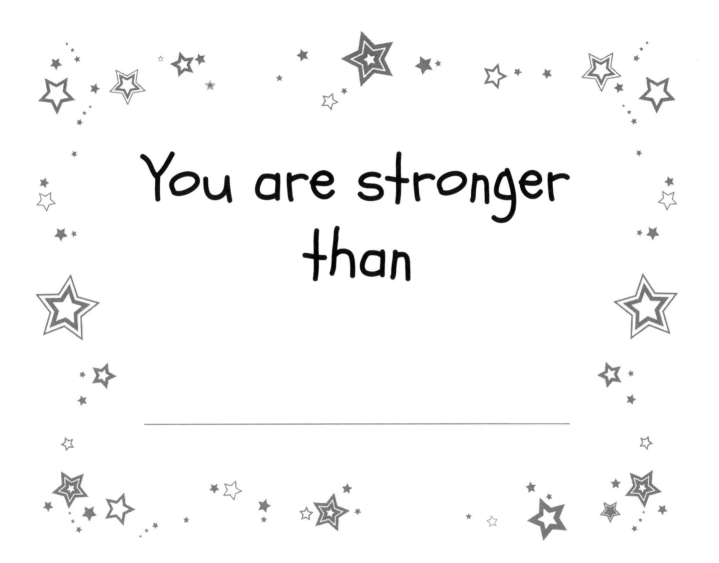

You are stronger than

_____

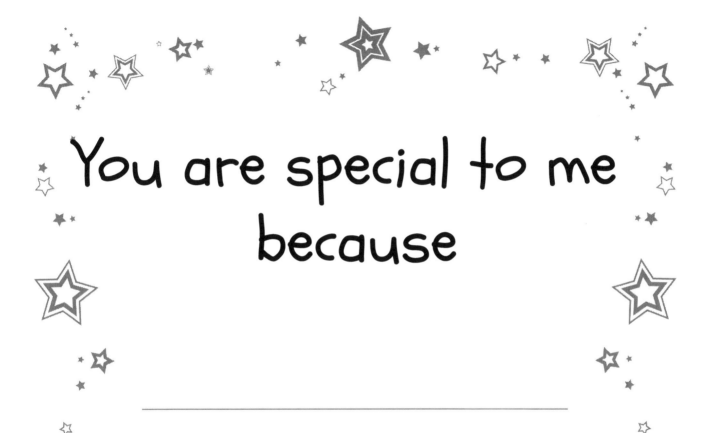

You are special to me because

_____

You make everyone

You taught me
how to

_____

I love when you tell stories about

_____

You inspire me
to do

_____

I enjoyed a lot when
we went to

_____

I love when we prank

_____

I love you a lot
because you never

_____

Funniest thing you do is

_____

I wish we have more time to

_____

I feel safe when you

_____

You don't care
about

_____

I like when you make funny

_____

I loved when you surprised me with

I love you
more than

_____

Game I like to play
with you is

_____

You are proud of me when I

_____

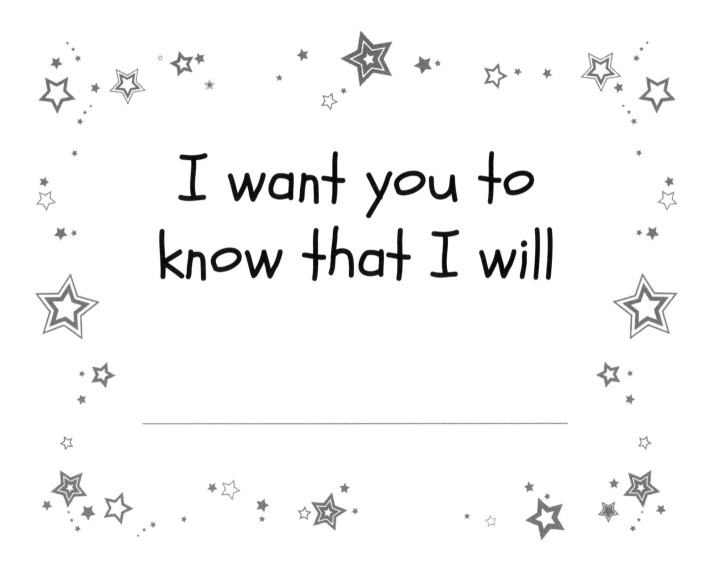

I want you to know that I will

_____

Made in the USA
Monee, IL
13 June 2023

35743788R00035